The Gospel of Nicodemus
or Acts of Pilate

based on public domain text.

MEMORIALS OF OUR LORD JESUS CHRIST DONE IN THE TIME OF PONTIUS PILATE

Prologue

(Absent from some manuscripts and versions).

I Ananias (Aeneas Copt., Emaus Lat.), the Protector, of praetorian rank, learned in the law, did from the divine scriptures recognize our Lord Jesus Christ and came near to him by faith and was accounted worthy of holy baptism: and I sought out the memorials that were made at that season in the time of our master Jesus Christ, which the Jews deposited with Pontius Pilate, and found the memorials in Hebrew (letters), and by the good pleasure of God I translated them into Greek (letters) for the informing of all them that call upon the name of our Lord Jesus Christ: in the reign of our Lord Flavius Theodosius, in the seventeenth year, and of Flavius Valentinianus the sixth, in the ninth indiction [corrupt: Lat. has the eighteenth year of Theodosius, when Valentinian was proclaimed Augustus, i. e. A. D. 425].

All ye therefore that read this and translate (or copy) it into other books, remember me and pray for me that God will be gracious unto me and be merciful unto my sins which I have sinned against him.

Peace be to them that read and that hear these things and to their servants. Amen.

In the fifteenth (al. nineteenth) year of the governance of Tiberius Caesar, emperor of the Romans, and of Herod, king of Galilee, in the nineteenth year of his rule, on the eighth of the Calends of April, which is the 25th of March, in the consulate of Rufus and Rubellio, in the fourth year of the two hundred and second Olympiad, Joseph who is Caiaphas being high priest of the Jews:

These be the things which after the cross and passion of the Lord Nicodemus recorded and delivered unto the high priest and the rest of the Jews: and the same Nicodemus set them forth in Hebrew (letters).

I

1 For the chief priests and scribes assembled in council, even Annas and Caiaphas and Somne (Senes) and Dothaim (Dothael, Dathaes, Datam) and Gamaliel, Judas, Levi and Nepthalim, Alexander and Jairus and the rest of the Jews, and came unto Pilate accusing Jesus for many deeds, saying: We know this man, that he is the son of Joseph the carpenter, begotten of Mary, and he saith that he is the Son of God and a king; more-over he doth pollute the sabbaths and he would destroy the law of our fathers.

Pilate saith: And what things are they that he doeth, and would destroy the law?

The Jews say: We have a law that we should not heal any man on the sabbath: but this man of his evil deeds hath healed the lame and the bent, the withered and the blind and the paralytic, the dumb and them that were possessed, on the sabbath day!

Pilate saith unto them: By what evil deeds?

They say unto him: He is a sorcerer, and by Beelzebub the prince of the devils he casteth out devils, and they are all subject unto him.

Pilate saith unto them: This is not to cast out devils by an unclean spirit, but by the god Asclepius.

2 The Jews say unto Pilate: We beseech thy majesty that he appear before thy judgement-seat and be heard. And Pilate called them unto him and said: Tell me, how can I that am a governor examine a king? They say unto him: We say not that he is a king, but he saith it of himself.

And Pilate called the messenger (cursor) and said unto him: Let Jesus be brought hither, but with gentleness. And the messenger went forth, and when he perceived Jesus he worshipped him and took the kerchief that was on his hand and spread it upon the earth and saith unto him: Lord, walk hereon and enter in, for the governor calleth thee. And when the Jews saw what the messenger had done, they cried out against Pilate saying: Wherefore didst thou not summon him by an herald to enter in, but by a messenger? for the messenger when he saw him worshipped him and spread out his kerchief upon the ground and hath made him walk upon it like a king!

3 Then Pilate called for the messenger and said unto him: Wherefore hast thou done this, and hast spread thy kerchief upon the ground and made Jesus to walk upon it? The messenger saith unto him: Lord governor, when thou sentest me to Jerusalem unto Alexander, I saw Jesus sitting upon an ass, and the children of the Hebrews held branches in their hands and cried out, and others spread their garments beneath him, saying: Save now, thou that art in the highest: blessed is he that cometh in the name of the Lord.

4 The Jews cried out and said unto the messenger: The children of the Hebrews cried out in Hebrew: how then hast thou it in the Greek? The messenger saith to them: I did ask one of the Jews and said: What is it that they cry out in Hebrew? and he interpreted it unto me.

Pilate saith unto them: And how cried they in Hebrew? The Jews say unto him: Hosanna membrome barouchamma adonai. Pilate saith unto them: And the Hosanna and the rest, how is it interpreted? The Jews say unto him: Save now, thou that art in the highest: blessed is he that cometh in the name of the Lord. Pilate saith unto them: If you yourselves bear witness of the words which were said of the children, wherein hath the messenger sinned? and they held their peace.

The governor saith unto the messenger: Go forth and bring him in after what manner thou wilt. And the messenger went forth and did after the former manner and said unto Jesus: Lord, enter in: the governor calleth thee.

5 Now when Jesus entered in, and the ensigns were holding the standards, the images (busts) of the standards bowed and did reverence to Jesus. And when the Jews saw the carriage of the standards, how they bowed themselves and did reverence unto Jesus, they cried out above measure against the ensigns. But Pilate said unto the Jews: Marvel ye not that the images bowed themselves and did reverence unto Jesus. The Jews say unto Pilate: We saw how the ensigns made them to bow and did reverence to him. And the governor called for the ensigns and saith unto them: Wherefore did ye so? They say unto Pilate: We are Greeks and servers of temples, and how could we do him reverence? for indeed, whilst we held the images they bowed of themselves and did reverence unto him.

6 Then saith Pilate unto the rulers of the synagogue and the elders of the people: Choose you out able and strong men and let them hold the standards, and let us see if they bow of themselves. And the elders of the Jews took twelve men strong and able and made them to hold the standards by sixes, and they were set before the judgement-seat of the

governor; and Pilate said to the messenger: Take him out of the judgement hall (praetorium) and bring him in again after what manner thou wilt. And Jesus went out of the judgement hall, he and the messenger. And Pilate called unto him them that before held the image and said unto them: I have sworn by the safety of Caesar that if the standards bow not when Jesus entereth in, I will cut off your heads.

And the governor commanded Jesus to enter in the second time. And the messenger did after the former manner and besought Jesus much that he would walk upon his kerchief; and he walked upon it and entered in. And when he had entered, the standards bowed themselves again and did reverence unto Jesus.

II

1 Now when Pilate saw it he was afraid, and sought to rise up from the judgement-seat. And while he yet thought to rise up, his wife sent unto him, saying: Have thou nothing to do with this just man, for I have suffered many things because of him by night. And Pilate called unto him all the Jews, and said unto them: Ye know that my wife feareth God and favoureth rather the customs of the Jews, with you? They say unto him: Yea, we know it. Pilate saith unto them: Lo, my wife hath sent unto me, saying: Have thou nothing to do with this just man: for I have suffered many things because of him by night. But the Jews answered and said unto Pilate: Said we not unto thee that he is a sorcerer? behold, he hath sent a vision of a dream unto thy wife.

2 And Pilate called Jesus unto him and said to him: What is it that these witness against thee? speakest thou nothing? But Jesus said: If they had not had power they would have

spoken nothing; for every man hath power over his own mouth, to speak good or evil: they shall see to it.

3 The elders of the Jews answered and said unto Jesus: What shall we see? Firstly, that thou wast born of fornication; secondly, that thy birth in Bethlehem was the cause of the slaying of children; thirdly, that thy father Joseph and thy mother Mary fled into Egypt because they had no confidence before the people.

4 Then said certain of them that stood by, devout men of the Jews: We say not that he came of fornication; but we know that Joseph was betrothed unto Mary, and he was not born of fornication. Pilate saith unto those Jews which said that he came of fornication: This your saying is not true for there were espousals, as these also say which are of your nation. Annas and Caiaphas say unto Pilate: The whole multitude of us cry out that he was born of fornication, and we are not believed: but these are proselytes and disciples of his. And Pilate called Annas and Caiaphas unto him and said to them: What be proselytes? They say unto him: They were born children of Greeks, and now are they become Jews. Then said they which said l that he was not born of fornication, even Lazarus, Asterius, Antonius, Jacob, Amnes, Zenas, Samuel, Isaac, Phinees, Crispus, Agrippa and Judas: We were not born proselytes (are not Greeks, Copt.), but we are children of Jews and we speak the truth; for verily we were present at the espousals of Joseph and Mary.

5 And Pilate called unto him those twelve men which said that he was not born of fornication, and saith unto them: I adjure you by the safety of Caesar, are these things true which ye have said, that he was not born of fornication? They say unto Pilate: We have a law that we swear not, because it is sin: But let them swear by the safety of Caesar

that it is not as we have said, and we will be guilty of death. Pilate saith to Annas and Caiaphas: Answer ye nothing to these things? Annas and Caiaphas say unto Pilate: These twelve men are believed which say that he was not born of fornication, but the whole multitude of us cry out that he was born of fornication, and is a sorcerer, and saith that he is the Son of God and a king, and we are not believed.

6 And Pilate commanded the whole multitude to go out, saving the twelve men which said that he was not born of fornication and he commanded Jesus to be set apart: and Pilate saith unto them: For what cause do they desire to put him to death? They say unto Pilate: They have jealousy, because he healeth on the sabbath day. Pilate saith: For a good work do they desire to put him to death? They say unto him: Yea.

III

1 And Pilate was filled with indignation and went forth without the judgement hall and saith unto them: I call the Sun to witness that I find no fault in this man. The Jews answered and said to the governor: If this man were not a malefactor we would not have delivered him unto thee. And Pilate said: Take ye him and judge him according to your law. The Jews said unto Pilate: It is not lawful for us to put any man to death. Pilate said: Hath God forbidden you to slay, and allowed me?

2 And Pilate went in again into the judgement hall and called Jesus apart and said unto him: Art thou the King of the Jews? Jesus answered and said to Pilate: Sayest thou this thing of thyself, or did others tell it thee of me? Pilate answered Jesus: Am I also a Jew? thine own nation and the chief priests have delivered thee unto me: what hast thou done? Jesus answered: My kingdom is not of this world; for

if my kingdom were of this world, my servants would have striven that I should not be delivered to the Jews: but now is my kingdom not from hence. Pilate said unto him: Art thou a king, then? Jesus answered him: Thou sayest that I am a king; for this cause was I born and am come, that every one that is of the truth should hear my voice. Pilate saith unto him: What is truth? Jesus saith unto him: Truth is of heaven. Pilate saith: Is there not truth upon earth? Jesus saith unto Pilate: Thou seest how that they which speak the truth are judged of them that have authority upon earth.

IV

1 And Pilate left Jesus in the judgement hall and went forth to the Jews and said unto them: I find no fault in him. The Jews say unto him: This man said: I am able to destroy this temple and in three days to build it up. Pilate saith: What temple? The Jews say: That which Solomon built in forty and six years but which this man saith he will destroy and build it in three days. Pilate saith unto them: I am guiltless of the blood of this just man: see ye to it. The Jews say: His blood be upon us and on our children.

2 And Pilate called the elders and the priests and Levites unto him and said to them secretly: Do not so: for there is nothing worthy of death whereof ye have accused him, for your accusation is concerning healing and profaning of the sabbath. The elders and the priests and Levites say: If a man blaspheme against Caesar, is he worthy of death or no? Pilate saith: He is worthy of death. The Jews say unto Pilate: If a man be worthy of death if he blaspheme against Caesar, this man hath blasphemed against God.

3 Then the governor commanded all the Jews to go out from the judgement hall, and he called Jesus to him and saith unto him: What shall I do with thee? Jesus saith unto

Pilate: Do as it hath been given thee. Pilate saith: How hath it been given? Jesus saith: Moses and the prophets did foretell concerning my death and rising again. Now the Jews inquired by stealth and heard, and they say unto Pilate: What needest thou to hear further of this blasphemy? Pilate saith unto the Jews: If this word be of blasphemy, take ye him for his blasphemy, and bring him into your synagogue and judge him according to your law. The Jews say unto Pilate: It is contained in our law, that if a man sin against a man, he is worthy to receive forty stripes save one: but he that blasphemeth against God, that he should be stoned with stoning.

4 Pilate saith unto them: Take ye him and avenge yourselves of him in what manner ye will. The Jews say unto Pilate: We will that he be crucified. Pilate saith: He deserveth not to be crucified.

5 Now as the governor looked round about upon the multitude of the Jews which stood by, he beheld many of the Jews weeping, and said: Not all the multitude desire that he should be put to death. The elder of the Jews said: To this end have the whole multitude of us come Hither, that he should be put to death. Pilate saith to the Jews: Wherefore should he die? The Jews said: Because he called himself the Son of God, and a king.

V

1 But a certain man, Nicodemus, a Jew, came and stood before the governor and said: I beseech thee, good (pious) lord, bid me speak a few words. Pilate saith: Say on. Nicodemus saith: I said unto the elders and the priests and Levites and unto all the multitude of the Jews in the synagogue: Wherefore contend ye with this man? This man doeth many and wonderful signs, which no man hath done,

neither will do: let him alone and contrive not any evil against him: if the signs which he doeth are of God, they will stand, but if they be of men, they will come to nought. For verily Moses, when he was sent of God into Egypt did many signs, which God commanded him to do before Pharaoh, king of Egypt; and there were there certain men servants of Pharaoh, Jannes and Jambres, and they also did signs not a few, of them which Moses did, and the Egyptians held them as gods, even Jannes and Jambres: and whereas the signs which they did were not of God, they perished and those also that believed on them. And now let this man go, for he is not worthy of death.

2 The Jews say unto Nicodemus: Thou didst become his disciple and thou speakest on his behalf. Nicodemus saith unto them: Is the governor also become his disciple, that he speaketh on his behalf? did not Caesar appoint him unto this dignity? And the Jews were raging and gnashing their teeth against Nicodemus. Pilate saith unto them: Wherefore gnash ye your teeth against him, wherens ye have heard the truth? The Jews say unto Nicodemus: Mayest thou receive his truth and his portion. Nicodemus saith: Amen, Amen: may I receive it as ye have said.

VI

1 Now one of the Jews came forward and besought the governor that he might speak a word. The governor saith: If thou wilt say aught, speak on. And the Jew said: Thirty and eight years lay I on a bed in suffering of pains, and at the coming of Jesus many that were possessed and laid with divers diseases were healed by him, and certain (faithful) young men took pity on me and carried me with my bed and brought me unto him; and when Jesus saw me he had compassion, and spake a word unto me: Take up thy bed and walk. And I took up my bed and walked. The Jews say

unto Pilate: Ask of him what day it was whereon he was healed? He that was healed saith: On the sabbath. The Jews say: Did we not inform thee so, that upon the sabbath he healeth and casteth out devils?

2 And another Jew came forward and said: I was born blind: I heard words but I saw no man's face: and as Jesus passed by I cried with a loud voice: Have mercy on me, O son of David. And he took pity on me and put his hands upon mine eyes and I received sight immediately. And another Jew came forward and said: I was bowed and he made me straight with a word. And another said: I was a leper, and he healed me with a word.

VII

And a certain woman named Bernice (Beronice Copt., Veronica Lat.) crying out from afar off said: I had an issue of blood and touched the hem of his garment, and the flowing of my blood was stayed which I had twelve years. The Jews say: We have a law that a woman shall not come to give testimony.

VIII

And certain others, even a multitude both of men and women cried out, saying: This man is a prophet and the devils are subject unto him. Pilate saith to them which said: The devils are subject unto him: Wherefore were not your teachers also subject unto him? They say unto Pilate: We know not. Others also said: He raised up Lazarus which was dead out of his tomb after four days. And the governor was afraid and said unto all the multitude of the Jews: Wherefore will ye shed innocent blood?

IX

1 And he called unto him Nicodemus and those twelve men which said that he was not born of fornication, and said unto them: What shall I do, for there riseth sedition among the people? They say unto him: We know not, let them see to it. Again Pilate called for all the multitude of the Jews and saith: Ye know that ye have a custom that at the feast of unleavened bread I should release unto you a prisoner. Now I have a prisoner under condemnation in the prison, a murderer, Barabbas by name, and this Jesus also which standeth before you, in whom I find no fault: Whom will ye that I release unto you? But they cried out: Barabbas. Pilate saith: What shall I do then with Jesus who is called Christ? The Jews say: Let him be crucified. But certain of the Jews answered: Thou art not a friend of Caesar's if thou let this man go; for he called himself the Son of God and a king: thou wilt therefore have him for king, and not Caesar.

2 And Pilate was wroth and said unto the Jews: Your nation is always seditious and ye rebel against your benefactors. The Jews say: Against what benefactors? Pilate saith: According as I have heard, your God brought you out of Egypt out of hard bondage, and led you safe through the sea as by dry land, and in the wilderness he nourished you with manna and gave you quails, and gave you water to drink out of a rock, and gave unto you a law. And in all these things ye provoked your God to anger, and sought out a molten calf, and angered your God and he sought to slay you: and Moses made supplication for you and ye were not put to death. And now ye do accuse me that I hate the king (emperor).

3 And he rose up from the judgement-seat and sought to go forth. And the Jews cried out, saying: We know our king, even Caesar and not Jesus. For indeed the wise men brought gifts from the east unto him as unto a king, and

when Herod heard from the wise men that a king was born, he sought to slay him, and when his father Joseph knew that, he took him and his mother and they fled into Egypt. And when Herod heard it he destroyed the children of the Hebrews that were born in Bethlehem.

4 And when Pilate heard these words he was afraid. And Pilate silenced the multitude, because they cried still, and said unto them: So, then, this is he whom Herod sought? The Jews say: Yea, this is he. And Pilate took water and washed his hands before the sun, saying: I am innocent of the blood of this just man: see ye to it. Again the Jews cried out: His blood be upon us and upon our children.

5 Then Pilate commanded the veil to be drawn before the judgement-seat whereon he sat, and saith unto Jesus: Thy nation hath convicted thee (accused thee) as being a king: therefore have I decreed that thou shouldest first be scourged according to the law of the pious emperors, and thereafter hanged upon the cross in the garden wherein thou wast taken: and let Dysmas and Gestas the two malefactors be crucified with thee.

X

1 And Jesus went forth of the judgement hall and the two malefactors with him. And when they were come to the place they stripped him of his garments and girt him with a linen cloth and put a crown of thorns about his head: likewise also they hanged up the two malefactors. But Jesus said: Father forgive them, for they know not what they do. And the soldiers divided his garments among them.

And the people stood looking upon him, and the chief priests and the rulers with them derided him, saying: He saved others let him save himself: if he be the son of God [let him come down from the cross]. And the soldiers also mocked him, coming and offering him vinegar with gall; and they said: If thou be the King of the Jews, save thyself.

And Pilate after the sentence commanded his accusation to be written for a title in letters of Greek and Latin and Hebrew according to the saying of the Jews: that he was the King of the Jews.

2 And one of the malefactors that were hanged [by name Gestas] spake unto him, saying: If thou be the Christ, save thyself, and us. But Dysmas answering rebuked him, saying: Dost thou not at all fear God, seeing thou art in the same condemnation? and we indeed justly, for we receive the due reward of our deeds; but this man hath done nothing amiss. And he said unto Jesus: Remember me, Lord, in thy kingdom. And Jesus said unto him: Verily, verily, I say unto thee, that today thou shalt be (art) with me in paradise.

XI

1 And it was about the sixth hour, and there was darkness over the land until the ninth hour, for the sun was darkened: and the veil of the temple was rent asunder in the midst. And Jesus called with a loud voice and said: Father, baddach ephkid rouel, which is interpreted: Into thy hands I commend my spirit. And having thus said he gave up the ghost. And when the centurion saw what was done, he glorified God, saying: This man was righteous. And all the multitudes that had come to the sight, when they beheld what was done smote their breasts and returned.

2 But the centurion reported unto the governor the things that had come to pass: and when the governor and his wife heard, they were sore vexed, and neither ate nor drank that

day. And Pilate sent for the Jews and said unto them: Did ye see that which came to pass? But they said: There was an eclipse of the sun after the accustomed sort.

3 And his acquaintance had stood afar off, and the women which came with him from Galilee, beholding these things. But a certain man named Joseph, being a counsellor, of the city of Arimathaea, who also himself looked for the kingdom of God this man went to Pilate and begged the body of Jesus. And he took it down and wrapped it in a clean linen cloth and laid it in a hewn sepulchre wherein was never man yet laid.

XII

1 Now when the Jews heard that Joseph had begged the body of Jesus, they sought for him and for the twelve men which said that Jesus was not born of fornication, and for Nicodemus and many others which had come forth before Pilate and declared his good works. But all they hid themselves, and Nicodemus only was seen of them, for he was a ruler of the Jews. And Nicodemus said unto them: How came ye into the synagogue? The Jews say unto him: How didst thou come into the synagogue? for thou art confederate with him, and his portion shall be with thee in the life to come. Nicodemus saith: Amen, Amen. Likewise Joseph also came forth and said unto them: Why is it that ye are vexed against me, for that I begged the body of Jesus? behold I have laid it in my new tomb, having wrapped it in clean linen, and I rolled a stone over the door of the cave. And ye have not dealt well with the just one, for ye repented not when ye had crucified him, but ye also pierced him with a spear.

But the Jews took hold on Joseph and commanded him to be put in safeguard until the first day of the week: and they said unto him: Know thou that the time alloweth us not to do anything against thee, because the sabbath dawneth: but knew that thou shalt not obtain burial, but we will give thy flesh unto the fowls of the heaven. Joseph saith unto them: This is the word of Goliath the boastful which reproached the living God and the holy David. For God said by the prophet: Vengeance is mine, and I will recompense, saith the Lord. And now, lo, one that was uncircumcised, but circumcised in heart, took water and washed his hands before the sun, saying: I am Innocent of the blood of this just person: see ye to it. And ye answered Pilate and said: His blood be upon us and upon our children. And now I fear lest the wrath of the Lord come upon you and upon your children, as ye have said. But when the Jews heard these words they waxed bitter in soul, and caught hold on Joseph and took him and shut him up in an house wherein was no window, and guards were set at the door: and they sealed the door of the place where Joseph was shut up.

2 And upon the sabbath day the rulers of the synagogue and the priests and the Levites made an ordinance that all men should appear in the synagogue on the first day of the week. And all the multitude rose up early and took council in the synagogue by what death they should kill him. And when the council was set they commanded him to be brought with great dishonour. And when they had opened the door they found him not. And all the people were beside themselves and amazed, because they found the seals closed, and Caiaphas had the key. And they durst not any more lay hands upon them that had spoken in the behalf of Jesus before Pilate.

XIII

1 And while they yet sat in the synagogue and marvelled because of Joseph, there came certain of the guard which

the Jews had asked of Pilate to keep the sepulchre of Jesus lest peradventure his disciples should come and steal him away. And they spake and declared unto the rulers of the synagogue and the priests and the Levites that which had come to pass: how that there was a great earthquake, and we saw an angel descend from heaven, and he rolled away the stone from the mouth of the cave, and sat upon it. And he did shine like snow and like lightning, and we were sore afraid and lay as dead men. And we heard the voice of the angel speaking with the women which waited at the sepulchre, saying: Fear ye not: for I know that ye seek Jesus which was crucified. He is not here: he is risen, as he said. Come, see the place where the Lord lay, and go quickly and say unto his disciples that he is risen from the dead, and is in Galilee.

2 The Jews say: With what women spake he? They of the guard say: We know not who they were. The Jews say: At what hour was it? They of the guard say: At midnight. The Jews say: And wherefore did ye not take the women? They of the guard say: We were become as dead me through fear, and we looked not to see the light of the day; how then could we take them? The Jews say: As the Lord liveth, we believe you not. They of the guard say unto the Jews: So many signs saw ye in that man, and ye believed not, how then should ye believe us? verily ye sware rightly 'as the Lord liveth', for he liveth indeed. Again they of the guard say: We have heard that ye shut up him that begged the body of Jesus, and that ye scaled the door; and when ye had opened it ye found him not. Give ye therefore Joseph and we will give you Jesus. The Jews say: Joseph is departed unto his own city. They of the guard say unto the Jews: Jesus also is risen, as we have heard of the angel, and he is in Galilee.

3 And when the Jews heard these words they were sore afraid, saying: Take heed lest this report be heard and all men incline unto Jesus. And the Jews took counsel and laid down much money and gave it to the soldiers, saying: Say ye: While we slept his disciples came by night and stole him away. And if this come to the governor's hearing we will persuade him and secure you. And they took the money and did as they were instructed. [And this their saying was published abroad among all men. lat.]

XIV

1 Now a certain priest named Phinees and Addas a teacher and Aggaeus (Ogias Copt., Egias lat.) a Levite came down from Galilee unto Jerusalem and told the rulers of the synagogue and the priests and the Levites, saying: We saw Jesus and his disciples sitting upon the mountain which is called Mamilch (Mambre or Malech lat., Mabrech Copt.), and he said unto his disciples: Go into all the world and preach unto every creature (the whole creation): he that believeth and is baptized shall be saved, but he that disbelieveth shall be condemned. [And these signs shall follow upon them that believe: in my name they shall cast out devils, they shall speak with new tongues, they shall take up serpents, and if they drink any deadly thing it shall not hurt them: they shall lay hands upon the sick and they shall recover.] And while Jesus yet spake unto his disciples we saw him taken up into heaven.

2 The elders and the priests and Levites say: Give glory to the God of Israel and make confession unto him: did ye indeed (or that ye did) hear and see those things which ye have told us? They that told them say: As the Lord God of our fathers Abraham, Isaac, and Jacob liveth, we did hear these things and we saw him taken up into heaven. The elders and the priests and the Levites say unto them: Came

ye for this end, that ye might tell us, or came ye to pay your vows unto God? And they say: To pay our vows unto God. The elders and the chief priests and the Levites say unto them: If ye came to pay your vows unto God, to what purpose is this idle tale which ye have babbled before all the people? Phinees the priest and Addas the teacher and Aggaeus the Levite say unto the rulers of the synagogue and priests and Levites: If these words which ye have spoken and seen be sin, lo, we are before you: do unto us as seemeth good in your eyes. And they took the book of the law and adjured them that they should no more tell any man these words: and they gave them to eat and to drink, and put them out of the city: moreover they gave them money, and three men to go with them, and they set them on their way as far as Galilee, and they departed in peace.

3 Now when these men were departed into Galilee, the chief priests and the rulers of the synagogue and the elders gathered together in the synagogue, and shut the gate, and lamented with a great lamentation, saying: What is this sign which is come to pass in Israel? But Amlas and Caiaphas said: Wherefore are ye troubled? why weep ye? Know ye not that his disciples gave much gold unto them that kept the sepulchre and taught them to say that an angel came down and rolled away the stone from the door of the sepulchre? But the priests and the elders said: Be it so, that his disciples did steal away his body; but how is his soul entered into his body, and how abideth he in Galilee? But they could not answer these things, and hardly in the end said: It is not lawful for us to believe the uncircumcised. [Lat. (and Copt., and Arm.): Ought we to believe the soldiers, that an angel came down from heaven and rolled away the stone from the door of the sepulchre? but in truth his disciples gave . . . sepulchre. Know ye not that it is not lawful for Jews to believe any word of the uncircumcised,

knowing that they who received much good from us have spoken according as we taught them.]

XV

And Nicodemus rose up and stood before the council, saying: Ye say well. Know ye not, O people of the Lord, the men that came down out of Galilee, that they fear God and are men of substance, hating covetousness (a lie, Lat.), men of peace? And they have told you with an oath, saying: We saw Jesus upon the mount Mamilch with his disciples and that he taught them all things that ye heard of them, and, say they, we saw him taken up into heaven. And no man asked them in what manner he was taken up. For like as the book of the holy scriptures hath taught us that Elias also was taken up into heaven, and Eliseus cried out with a loud voice, and Elias cast his hairy cloak upon Eliseus, and Eliseus cast the cloak upon Jordan and passed over and went unto Jericho. And the sons of the prophets met him and said: Eliseus, where is thy lord Elias? and he said that he was taken up into heaven. And they said unto Eliseus: Hath not a spirit caught him up and cast him upon one of the mountains? but let us take our servants with us and seek after him. And they persuaded Eliseus and he went with them, and they sought him three days and found him not: and they knew that he had been taken up. And now hearken unto me, and let us send into all the coasts (al. mountains) of Israel and see whether the Christ were not taken up by a spirit and cast upon one of the mountains. And this saying pleased them all: and they sent into all the coasts (mountains, Lat.) and sought Jesus and found him not. But they found Joseph in Arimathaea, and no man durst lay hands upon him.

2 And they told the elders and the priests and the Levites, saying: We went about throughout all the coasts of Israel,

and we found not Jesus; but Joseph we found in Arimathaea. And when they heard of Joseph they rejoiced and gave glory to the God of Israel. And the rulers of the synagogue and the priests and the Levites took counsel how they should meet with Joseph, and they took a volume of paper and wrote unto Joseph these words:

Peace be unto thee. We know that we have sinned against God and against thee, and we have prayed unto the God of Israel that thou shouldest vouchsafe to come unto thy fathers and unto thy children (Lat. But thou didst pray unto the God of Israel, and he delivered thee out of our hands. Now therefore vouchsafe, &c.) for we are all troubled, because when we opened the door we found thee not: and we know that we devised an evil counsel against thee, but the Lord helped thee. And the Lord himself made of none effect (scattered) our counsel against thee, O father Joseph, thou that art honourable among all the people.

3 And they chose out of all Israel seven men that were friends of Joseph, whom Joseph also himself accounted his friends, and the rulers of the synagogue and the priests and the Levites said unto them: See: if he receive our epistle and read it, know that he will come with you unto us: but if he read it not, know that he is vexed with us, and salute ye him in peace and return unto us. And they blessed the men and let them go.

And the men came unto Joseph and did him reverence, and said unto him: Peace be unto thee. And he said: Peace be unto you and unto all the people of Israel. And they gave him the book of the epistle, and Joseph received it and read it and embraced (or kissed) the epistle and blessed God and said: Blessed be the Lord God, which hath redeemed Israel from shedding innocent blood; and blessed be the Lord, which sent his angel and sheltered me under his wings.

(And he kissed them) and set a table before them, and they did eat and drink and lay there.

4 And they rose up early and prayed: and Joseph saddled his she-ass and went with the men, and they came unto the holy city, even Jerusalem. And all the people came to meet Joseph and cried: Peace be to thine entering-in. And he said unto all the people: Peace be unto you, and all the people kissed him. And the people prayed with Joseph, and they were astonished at the sight of him.

And Nicodemus received him into his house and made a great feast, and called Annas and Caiaphas and the elders and the priests and the Levites unto his house. And they made merry eating and drinking with Joseph. And when they had sung an hymn (or blessed God) every man went unto his house. But Joseph abode in the house of Nicodemus.

5 And on the morrow, which was the preparation, the rulers of the synagogue and the priests and the Levites rose up early and came to the house of Nicodemus, and Nicodemus met them and said: Peace be unto you. And they said: Peace be unto thee and to Joseph and unto all thy house and to all the house of Joseph. And he brought them into his house. And the whole council was set, and Joseph sat between Annas and Caiaphas and no man durst speak unto him a word. And Joseph said: Why is it that ye have called me? And they beckoned unto Nicodemus that he should speak unto Joseph. And Nicodemus opened his mouth and said unto Joseph: Father, thou knowest that the reverend doctors and the priests and the Levites seek to learn a matter of thee. And Joseph said: Inquire ye. And Annas and Caiaphas took the book of the law and adjured Joseph saying: Give glory to the God of Israel and make confession unto him: [for Achar, when he was adjured of

the prophet Jesus(Joshua), foreswore not himself but declared unto him all things and hid not a word from him: thou therefore also hide not from us so much as a word. And Joseph: I will not hide one word from you.] And they said unto him: We were greatly vexed because thou didst beg the body of Jesus and wrappedst it in a clean linen cloth and didst lay him in a tomb. And for this cause we put thee in safeguard in an house wherein was no window, and we put keys and seals upon the doors, and guards did keep the place wherein thou wast shut up. And on the first day of the week we opened it and found thee not, and we were sore troubled, and amazement fell upon all the people of the Lord until yesterday. Now, therefore, declare unto us what befell thee.

6 And Joseph said: On the preparation day about the tenth hour ye did shut me up, and I continued there the whole sabbath. And at midnight as I stood and prayed the house wherein ye shut me up was taken up by the four corners, and I saw as it were a flashing of light in mine eyes, and being filled with fear I fell to the earth. And one took me by the hand and removed me from the place whereon I had fallen; and moisture of water was shed on me from my head unto my feet, and an odour of ointment came about my nostrils. And he wiped my face and kissed me and said unto me: Fear not, Joseph: open thine eyes and see who it is that speaketh with thee. And I looked up and saw Jesus and I trembled, and supposed that it was a spirit: and I said the commandments: and he said them with me. And [as] ye are not ignorant that a spirit, if it meet any man and hear the commandments, straightway fleeth. And when I perceived that he said them with me, I said unto him: Rabbi Elias? And he said unto me: I am not Elias. And I said unto him: Who art thou, Lord? And he said unto me: I am Jesus, whose body thou didst beg of Pilate, and didst clothe me in

clean linen and cover my face with a napkin, and lay me in thy new cave and roll a great stone upon the door of the cave. And I said to him that spake with me: Show me the place where I laid thee. And he brought me and showed me the place where I laid him, and the linen cloth lay therein, and the napkin that was upon his face. And I knew that it was Jesus. And he took me by the hand and set me in the midst of mine house, the doors being shut, and laid me upon my bed and said unto me: Peace be unto thee. And he kissed me and said unto me: Until forty days be ended go not out of thine house: for behold I go unto my brethren into Galilee.

XVI

1 And when the rulers of the synagogue and the priests and the Levites heard these words of Joseph the became as dead men and fell to the ground, and they fasted until the ninth hour. And Nicodemus with Joseph comforted Annas and Caiaphas and the priests and the Levites, saying: Rise up and stand on your feet and taste bread and strengthen your souls, for tomorrow is the sabbath of the Lord. And they rose up and prayed unto God and did eat and drink, and departed every man to his house.

2 And on the sabbath the (al. our) teachers and the priests and Levites sat and questioned one another and said: What is this wrath that is come upon us? for we know his father and his mother. Levi the teacher saith: I know that his parents feared God and kept not back their vows and paid tithes three times a year. And when Jesus was born, his parents brought him up unto this place and gave sacrifices and burnt-offerings to God. And [when] the great teacher Symeon took him into his arms and said: Now lettest thou thy servant, Lord, depart in peace for mine eyes have seen thy salvation which thou hast prepared before the face of all

peoples, a light to lighten the Gentiles and the glory of thy people Israel. And Symeon blessed them and said unto Mary his mother: I give thee good tidings concerning this child. And Mary said: Good, my lord? And Symeon said to her : Good. Behold, he is set for the fall and rising again of many in Israel, and for a sign spoken against: and a sword shall pierce through thine own heart also, that the thoughts of many hearts may be revealed.

3 They say unto Levi the teacher: How knowest thou these things? Levi saith unto them: Know ye not that from him I did learn the law? The council say unto him: We would see thy father. And they sent after his father, and asked of him, and he said to them: Why believed ye not my son? the blessed and righteous Symeon, he did teach him the law. The council saith: Rabbi Levi, is the word true which thou hast spoken? And he said: It is true.

Then the rulers of the synagogue and the priests and the Levites said among themselves: Come, let us send into Galilee unto the three men which came and told us of his teaching and his taking-up, and let them tell us how they saw him taken up. And this word pleased them all, and they sent the three men which before had gone with them into Galilee and said to them: Say unto Rabbi Addas and Rabbi Phinees and Rabbi Aggaeus: peace be to you and to all that are with you. Inasmuch as great questioning hath arisen in the council, we have sent unto you to call you unto this holy place of Jerusalem.

4 And the men went into Galilee and found them sitting and meditating upon the law, and saluted them in peace. And the men that were in Galilee said unto them that were come to them: Peace be upon all Israel. And they said: Peace be unto you. Again they said unto them: Wherefore are ye come? And they that were sent said: The council

calleth you unto the holy city Jerusalem. And when the men heard that they were bidden by the council, they prayed to God and sat down to meat with the men and did eat and drink, and rose up and came in peace unto Jerusalem.

5 And on the morrow the council was set in the synagogue, and they examined them, saying: Did ye in very deed see Jesus sitting upon the mount Mamilch, as he taught his eleven disciples, and saw ye him taken up? And the men answered them and said: Even as we saw him taken up, even so did we tell it unto you.

6 Annas saith: Set them apart from one another, and let us see if their word agreeth. And they set them apart one from another, and they call Addas first and say unto him: How sawest thou Jesus taken up? Addas saith: While he yet sat upon the Mount Mamilch and taught his disciples, we saw a cloud that overshadowed him and his disciples: and the cloud carried him up into heaven, and his disciples lay (al. prayed, lying) on their faces upon the earth. And they called Phinees the priest, and questioned him also, saying: How sawest thou Jesus taken up? And he spake in like manner. And again they asked Aggaeus, and he also spake in like manner. And the council said: It is contained in the law of Moses: At the mouth of two or three shall every word be established.

Abuthem (Bouthem Gr., Abudem lat., Abuden, Abuthen Arm.,om. Copt.) the teacher saith: It is written in the law: Enoch walked with God and is not, because God took him. Jaeirus the teacher said: Also we have heard of the death of the holy Moses and have not seen him; for it is written in the law of the Lord: And Moses died at the mouth of the Lord, and no man knew of his sepulchre unto this day. And Rabbi Levi said: Wherefore was it that Rabbi Symeon said when he saw Jesus: Behold, this child is set for the fall and rising again of many in Israel and for a sign spoken against? And Rabbi Isaac said: It is written in the law: Behold I send my messenger before thy face, which shall go before thee to keep thee in every good way, for my name is named thereon.

7 Then said Annas and Caiaphas: Ye have well said those things which are written in the law of Moses, that no man saw the death of Enoch, and no man hath named the death of Moses. But Jesus spake before Pilate, and we know that we saw him receive buffets and spittings upon his face, and that the soldiers put on him a crown of thorns and that he was scourged and received condemnation from Pilate, and that he was crucified at the place of a skull and two thieves with him, and that they gave him vinegar to drink with gall, and that Longinus the soldier pierced his side with a spear, and that Joseph our honourable father begged his body, and that, as he saith, he rose again, and that (lit. as) the three teachers say: We saw him taken up into heaven, and that Rabbi Levi spake and testified to the things which were spoken by Rabbi Symeon, and that he said: Behold this child is set for the fall and rising again of many in Israel and for a sign spoken against.

And all the teachers said unto all the people of the Lord: If this hath come to pass from the Lord, and it is marvelous in our eyes, ye shall surely know, O house of Jacob, that it is written: Cursed is every one that hangeth upon a tree. And another scripture teacheth: The gods which made not the heaven and the earth shall perish.

And the priests and the Levites said one to another: If his memorial endure until the Sommos (Copt. Soum) which is called Jobel (i. e. the Jubilee), know ye that he will prevail for ever and raise up for himself a new people.

Then the rulers of the synagogue and the priests and the Levites admonished all Israel, saying: Cursed is that man who shall worship that which man's hand hath made, and cursed is the man who shall worship creatures beside the Creator. And all the people said: Amen, Amen.

And all the people sang an hymn unto the Lord and said: Blessed be the Lord who hath given rest unto the people of Israel according to all that he spake. There hath not one word fallen to the ground of all his good saying which he spake unto his servant Moses. The Lord our God be with us as he was with our fathers: let him not forsake us. And let him not destroy us from turning our heart unto him, from walking in all his ways and keeping his statutes and his judgements which he commanded our fathers. And the Lord shall be King over all the earth in that day. And there shall be one Lord and his name one, even the Lord our King: he shall save us.

There is none like unto thee, O Lord. Great art thou, O Lord, and great is thy name.

Heal us, O Lord, by thy power, and we shall be healed: save us, Lord, and we shall be saved: for we are thy portion and thine inheritance.

And the Lord will not forsake his people for his great name's sake, for the Lord hath begun to make us to be his people.

And when they had all sung this hymn they departed every man to his house, glorifying God. [For his is the glory, world without end. Amen.]

ACTS OF PILATE

PART II. THE DESCENT INTO HELL

This writing, or the nucleus of it, the story of the Descent into Hell was not originally part of the Acts of Pilate. It is - apart from its setting- probably an older document. When it was first attached to the Acts of Pilate is uncertain. The object of this prefatory note is to say that we have the text in three forms, [however, only the Latin A text will be given. For a complete listing of all three texts see M.R. James apocryphal New Testament].

.[Part I, cap. xvi, ends with words of the rulers of the synagogue, &c. All nations shall serve him, and kings shall come from afar worshipping and magnifying him. Part II, cap. i, runs on from this.

I (XVII)

1 And Joseph arose and said unto Annas and Caiaphas: Truly and of right do ye marvel because ye have heard that Jesus hath been seen alive after death, and that he hath ascended into heaven. Nevertheless it is more marvelous that he rose not alone from the dead, but did raise up alive many other dead out of their sepulchres, and they have been seen of many in Jerusalem. And now hearken unto me; for we all know the blessed Simeon, the high priest which received the child Jesus in his hands in the temple. And this Simeon had two sons, brothers in blood and we all were at their falling asleep and at their burial. Go therefore and look upon their sepulchres: for they are open, because they have risen, and behold they are in the city of Arimathaea dwelling together in prayer. And indeed men hear them crying out, yet they speak with no man, but are silent as dead men. But come, let us go unto them and with all honour and gentleness bring them unto us, and if we adjure them, perchance they will tell us concerning the mystery of their rising again.

2 When they heard these things, they all rejoiced. And Annas and Caiaphas, Nicodemus and Joseph and Gamaliel went and found them not in their sepulchre, but they went unto the city of Arimathaea, and found them there, kneeling on their knees and giving themselves unto prayer. And they kissed them, and with all reverence and in the fear of God they brought them to Jerusalem into the synagogue. And they shut the doors and took the law of the Lord and put it into their hands, and adjured them by the God Adonai and the God of Israel which spake unto our fathers by the prophets, saying: Believe ye that it is Jesus which raised you from the dead? Tell us how ye have arisen from the dead.

3 And when Karinus and Leucius heard this adjuration, they trembled in their body and groaned, being troubled in heart. And looking up together unto heaven they made the seal of the cross with their fingers upon their tongues, and forthwith they spake both of them, saying: Give us each a volume of paper, and let us write that which we have seen and heard. And they gave them unto them, and each of them sat down and wrote, saying:

II (XVIII)

1 O Lord Jesu Christ, the life and resurrection of the dead (al. resurrection of the dead and the life of the living), suffer us to speak of the mysteries of thy majesty which thou didst perform after thy death upon the cross, inasmuch as we have been adjured by thy Name. For thou didst command us thy servants to tell no man the secrets of thy divine majesty which thou wroughtest in hell.

Now when we were set together with all our fathers in the deep, in obscurity of darkness, on a sudden there came a golden heat of the sun and a purple and royal light shining upon us. And immediately the father of the whole race of men, together with all the patriarchs and prophets, rejoiced, saying: This light is the beginning (author) of everlasting light which did promise to send unto us his co-eternal light. And Esaias cried out and said: This is the light of the Father, even the Son of God, according as I prophesied when I lived upon the earth: The land of Zabulon and the land of Nephthalim beyond Jordan, of Galilee of the Gentiles, the people that walked in darkness have seen a great light, and they that dwell in the land of the shadow of death, upon them did the light shine. And now hath it come and shone upon us that sit in death.

2 And as we all rejoiced in the light which shined upon us, there came unto us our father Simeon, and he rejoicing said unto us: Glorify ye the Lord Jesus Christ, the Son of God; for I received him in my hands in the temple when he was born a child, and being moved of the Holy Ghost I made confession and said unto him: Now have mine eyes seen thy salvation which thou hast prepared before the face of all people, a light to lighten the Gentiles, and to be the glory of thy people Israel. And when they heard these things, the whole multitude of the saints rejoiced yet more.

Page 125

3 And after that there came one as it were a dweller in the wilderness, and he was inquired of by all: Who art thou? And he answered them and said: I am John, the voice and the prophet of the most High, which came before the face of his advent to prepare his ways, to give knowledge of salvation unto his people, for the remission of their sins. And when I saw him coming unto me, being moved of the Holy Ghost, I said: Behold the Lamb of God, behold him that taketh away the sins of the world. And I baptized him in the river of Jordan, and saw the Holy Ghost descending

upon him in the likeness of a dove, and heard a voice out of heaven saying: This is my beloved Son, in whom I am well pleased. And now have I come before his face, and come down to declare unto you that he is at hand to visit us, even the day spring, the Son of God, coming from on high unto us that sit in darkness and in the shadow of death.

III (XIX)

1 And when father Adam that was first created heard this, even that Jesus was baptized in Jordan, he cried out to Seth his son, saying: Declare unto thy sons the patriarchs and the prophets all that thou didst hear from Michael the archangel, when I sent thee unto the gates of paradise that thou mightest entreat God to send thee his angel to give thee the oil of the tree of mercy to anoint my body when I was sick. Then Seth drew near unto the holy patriarchs and prophets, and said: When I, Seth, was praying at the gates of paradise, behold Michael the angel of the Lord appeared unto me, saying: I am sent unto thee from the Lord: it is I that am set over the body of man. And I say unto thee, Seth, vex not thyself with tears, praying and entreating for the oil of the tree of mercy, that thou mayest anoint thy father Adam for the pain of his body: for thou wilt not be able to receive it save in the last days and times, save when five thousand and five hundred (al. 5,952) years are accomplished: then shall the most beloved Son of God come upon the earth to raise up the body of Adam and the bodies of the dead, and he shall come and be baptized in Jordan. And when he is come forth of the water of Jordan, then shall he anoint with the oil of mercy all that believe on him, and that oil of mercy shall be unto all generations of them that shall be born of water and of the Holy Ghost, unto life eternal. Then shall the most beloved Son of God, even Christ Jesus, come down upon the earth and shall

bring in our father Adam into paradise unto the tree of mercy.

And when they heard all these things of Seth, all the patriarchs and prophets rejoiced with a great rejoicing.

IV (XX)

1 And while all the saints were rejoicing, behold Satan the prince and chief of death said unto Hell: Make thyself ready to receive Jesus who boasteth himself that he is the Son of God, whereas he is a man that feareth death, and sayeth: My soul is sorrowful even unto death. And he hath been much mine enemy, doing me great hurt, and many that I had made blind, lame, dumb, leprous, and possessed he hath healed with a word: and some whom I have brought unto thee dead, them hath he taken away from thee.

2 Hell answered and said unto Satan the prince: Who is he that is so mighty, if he be a man that feareth death? for all the mighty ones of the earth are held in subjection by my power, even they whom thou hast brought me subdued by thy power. If, then, thou art mighty, what manner of man is this Jesus who, though he fear death, resisteth thy power? If he be so mighty in his manhood, verily I say unto thee he is almighty in his god-head, and no man can withstand his power. And when he saith that he feareth death, he would ensnare thee, and woe shall be unto thee for everlasting ages. But Satan the prince of Tartarus said: Why doubtest thou and fearest to receive this Jesus which is thine adversary and mine? For I tempted him, and have stirred up mine ancient people of the Jews with envy and wrath against him. I have sharpened a spear to thrust him through, gall and vinegar have I mingled to give him to drink, and I have prepared a cross to crucify him and nails to pierce

him: and his death is nigh at hand, that I may bring him unto thee to be subject unto thee and me.

3 Hell answered and said: Thou hast told me that it is he that hath taken away dead men from me. For there be many which while they lived on the earth have taken dead men from me, yet not by their own power but by prayer to God, and their almighty God hath taken them from me. Who is this Jesus which by his own word without prayer hath drawn dead men from me? Perchance it is he which by the word of his command did restore to life Lazarus which was four days dead and stank and was corrupt, whom I held here dead. Satan the prince of death answered and said: It is that same Jesus. When Hell heard that he said unto him: I adjure thee by thy strength and mine own that thou bring him not unto me. For at that time I, when I heard the command of his word, did quake and was overwhelmed with fear, and all my ministries with me were troubled. Neither could we keep Lazarus, but he like an eagle shaking himself leaped forth with all agility and swiftness, and departed from us, and the earth also which held the dead body of Lazarus straightway gave him up alive. Wherefore now I know that that man which was able to do these things is a God strong in command and mighty in manhood, and that he is the saviour of mankind. And if thou bring him unto me he will set free all that are here shut up in the hard prison and bound in the chains of their sins that cannot be broken, and will bring them unto the life of his god head for ever.

V (XXI)

1 And as Satan the prince, and Hell, spoke this together, suddenly there came a voice as of thunder and a spiritual cry: Remove, O princes, your gates, and be ye lift up, ye everlasting doors, and the King of glory shall come in.

When Hell heard that he said unto Satan the prince: Depart from me and go out of mine abode: if thou be a mighty man of war, fight thou against the King of glory. But what hast thou to do with him? And Hell cast Satan forth out of his dwelling. Then said Hell unto his wicked ministers: Shut ye the hard gates of brass and put on them the bars of iron and withstand stoutly, lest we that hold captivity be taken captive.

2 But when all the multitude of the saints heard it, they spake with a voice of rebuking unto Hell: Open thy gates, that the King of glory may come in. And David cried out, saying: Did I not when I was alive upon earth, foretell unto you: Let them give thanks unto the Lord, even his mercies and his wonders unto the children of men; who hath broken the gates of brass and smitten the bars of iron in sunder? he hath taken them out of the way of their iniquity. And thereafter in like manner Esaias said: Did not I when I was alive upon earth foretell unto you: The dead shall arise, and they that are in the tombs shall rise again, and they that are in the earth shall rejoice, for the dew which cometh of the Lord is their healing? And again I said: O death, where is thy sting? O Hell, where is thy victory?

3 When they heard that of Esaias, all the saints said unto Hell: Open thy gates: now shalt thou be overcome and weak and without strength. And there came a great voice as of thunder, saying: Remove, O princes, your gates, and be ye lift up ye doors of hell, and the King of glory shall come in. And when Hell saw that they so cried out twice, he said, as if he knew it not: Who is the King of glory? And David answered Hell and said: The words of this cry do I know, for by his spirit I prophesied the same; and now I say unto thee that which I said before: The Lord strong and mighty, the Lord mighty in battle, he is the King of glory. And: The

Lord looked down from heaven that he might hear the groanings of them that are in fetters and deliver the children of them that have been slain. And now, O thou most foul and stinking Hell, open thy gates, that the King of glory may come in. And as David spake thus unto Hell, the Lord of majesty appeared in the form of a man and lightened the eternal darkness and brake the bonds that could not be loosed: and the succour of his everlasting might visited us that sat in the deep darkness of our transgressions and in the shadow of death of our sins.

VI (XXII)

1 When Hell and death and their wicked ministers saw that, they were stricken with fear, they and their cruel officers, at the sight of the brightness of so great light in their own realm, seeing Christ of a sudden in their abode, and they cried out, saying: We are overcome by thee. Who art thou that art sent by the Lord for our confusion? Who art thou that without all damage of corruption, and with the signs (?) of thy majesty unblemished, dost in wrath condemn our power? Who art thou that art so great and so small, both humble and exalted, both soldier and commander, a marvelous warrior in the shape of a bondsman, and a King of glory dead and living, whom the cross bare slain upon it? Thou that didst lie dead in the sepulchre hast come down unto us living and at thy death all creation quaked and all the stars were shaken and thou hast become free among the dead and dost rout our legions. Who art thou that settest free the prisoners that are held bound by original sin and restorest them into their former liberty? Who art thou that sheddest thy divine and bright light upon them that were blinded with the darkness of their sins? After the same manner all the legions of devils were stricken with like fear and cried out all together in the terror of their confusion,

saying: Whence art thou, Jesus, a man so mighty and bright in majesty, so excellent without spot and clean from sin? For that world of earth which hath been always subject unto us until now, and did pay tribute to our profit, hath never sent unto us a dead man like thee, nor ever dispatched such a gift unto Hell. Who then art thou that so fearlessly enterest our borders, and not only fearest not our torments, but besides essayest to bear away all men out of our bonds? Peradventure thou art that Jesus, of whom Satan our prince said that by thy death of the cross thou shouldest receive the dominion of the whole world.

2 Then did the King of glory in his majesty trample upon death, and laid hold on Satan the prince and delivered him unto the power of Hell, and drew Adam to him unto his own brightness.

VII (XXIII)

Then Hell, receiving Satan the prince, with sore reproach said unto him: O prince of perdition and chief of destruction, Beelzebub, the scorn of the angels and spitting of the righteous why wouldest thou do this? Thou wouldest crucify the King of glory and at his decease didst promise us great spoils of his death: like a fool thou knewest not what thou didst. For behold now, this Jesus putteth to flight by the brightness of his majesty all the darkness of death, and hath broken the strong depths of the prisons, and let out the prisoners and loosed them that were bound. And all that were sighing in our torments do rejoice against us, and at their prayers our dominions are vanquished and our realms conquered, and now no nation of men feareth us any more. And beside this, the dead which were never wont to be proud triumph over us, and the captives which never could be joyful do threaten us. O prince Satan, father of all the wicked and ungodly and renegades wherefore wouldest thou do this? They that from the beginning until now have despaired of life and salvation-now is none of their wonted roarings heard, neither doth any groan from them sound in our ears, nor is there any sign of tears upon the face of any of them. O prince Satan, holder of the keys of hell, those thy riches which thou hadst gained by the tree of transgression and the losing of paradise, thou hast lost by the tree of the cross, and all thy gladness hath perished. When thou didst hang up Christ Jesus the King of glory thou wroughtest against thyself and against me. Henceforth thou shalt know what eternal torments and infinite pains thou art to suffer in my keeping for ever. O prince Satan, author of death and head of all pride, thou oughtest first to have sought out matter of evil in this Jesus: Wherefore didst thou adventure without cause to crucify him unjustly against whom thou foundest no blame, and to bring into our realm the innocent and righteous one, and to lose the guilty and the ungodly and unrighteous of the whole world? And when Hell had spoken thus unto Satan the prince, then said the King of glory unto Hell: Satan the prince shall be in thy power unto all ages in the stead of Adam and his children, even those that are my righteous ones.

VIII (XXIV)

1 And the Lord stretching forth his hand, said: Come unto me, all ye my saints which bear mine image and my likeness. Ye that by the tree and the devil and death were condemned, behold now the devil and death condemned by the tree. And forthwith all the saints were gathered in one under the hand of the Lord. And the Lord holding the right hand of Adam, said unto him: Peace be unto thee with all thy children that are my righteous ones. But Adam, casting himself at the knees of the Lord entreated him with tears and beseechings, and said with a loud voice: I will magnify

thee, O Lord, for thou hast set me up and not made my foes to triumph over me: O Lord my God I cried unto thee and thou hast healed me; Lord, thou hast brought my soul out of hell, thou hast delivered me from them that go down to the pit. Sing praises unto the Lord all ye saints of his, and give thanks unto him for the remembrance of his holiness. For there is wrath in his indignation and life is in his good pleasure. In like manner all the saints of God kneeled and cast themselves at the feet of the Lord, saying with one accord: Thou art come, O redeemer of the world: that which thou didst foretell by the law and by thy prophets, that hast thou accomplished in deed. Thou hast redeemed the living by thy cross, and by the death of the cross thou hast come down unto us, that thou mightest save us out of hell and death through thy majesty. O Lord, like as thou hast set the name of thy glory in the heavens and set up thy cross for a token of redemption upon the earth, so, Lord, set thou up the sign of the victory of thy cross in hell, that death may have no more dominion.

2 And the Lord stretched forth his hand and made the sign of the cross over Adam and over all his saints, and he took the right hand of Adam and went up out of hell, and all the saints followed him. Then did holy David cry aloud and say: Sing unto the Lord a new song, for he hath done marvelous things. His right hand hath wrought salvation for him and his holy arm. The Lord hath made known his saving health, before the face of all nations hath he revealed his righteousness. And the whole multitude of the saints answered, saying: Such honour have all his saints. Amen, Alleluia.

3 And thereafter Habacuc the prophet cried out and said: Thou wentest forth for the salvation of thy people to set free thy chosen. And all the saints answered, saying:

Blessed is he that cometh in the name of the Lord. God is the Lord and hath showed us light. Amen, Alleluia. Likewise after that the prophet Micheas also cried, saying: What God is like thee, O Lord, taking away iniquity and removing sins? and now thou withholdest thy wrath for a testimony that thou art merciful of free will, and thou dost turn away and have mercy on us, thou forgivest all our iniquities and hast sunk all our sins in the depths of the sea, as thou swarest unto our fathers in the days of old. And all the saints answered, saying: This is our God for ever and ever, he shall be our guide, world without end. Amen, Alleluia. And so spake all the prophets, making mention of holy words out of their praises, and all the saints followed the Lord, crying Amen, Alleluia.

IX (XXV)

But the Lord holding the hand of Adam delivered him unto Michael the archangel, and all the saints followed Michael the archangel, and he brought them all into the glory and beauty (grace) of paradise. And there met with them two men, ancients of days, and when they were asked of the saints: Who are ye that have not yet been dead in hell with us and are set in paradise in the body? then one of them answering, said: I am Enoch which was translated hither by the word of the Lord, and this that is with me is Elias the Thesbite which was taken up in a chariot of fire: and up to this day we have not tasted death, but we are received unto the coming of Antichrist to fight against him with signs and wonders of God, and to be slain of him in Jerusalem, and after three days and a half to be taken up again alive on the clouds.

X (XXVI)

And as Enoch and Elias spake thus with the saints, behold there came another man of vile habit, bearing upon his shoulders the sign of the cross; whom when they beheld, all the saints said unto him: Who art thou? for thine appearance is as of a robber; and wherefore is it that thou bearest a sign upon thy shoulders? And he answered them and said: Ye have rightly said: for I was a robber, doing all manner of evil upon the earth. And the Jews crucified me with Jesus, and I beheld the wonders in the creation which came to pass through the cross of Jesus when he was crucified, and I believed that he was the maker of all creatures and the almighty king, and I besought him, saying: Remember me, Lord, when thou comest into thy kingdom. And forthwith he received my prayer, and said unto me: Verily I say unto thee, this day shalt thou be with me in paradise: and he gave me the sign of the cross, saying: Bear this and go unto paradise, and if the angel that keepeth paradise suffer thee not to enter in, show him the sign of the cross; and thou shalt say unto him: Jesus Christ the Son of God who now is crucified hath sent me. And when I had so done, I spake all these things unto the angel that keepeth paradise; and when he heard this of me, forthwith he opened the door and brought me in and set me at the right hand of paradise, saying: Lo now, tarry a little, and Adam the father of all mankind will enter in with all his children that are holy and righteous, after the triumph and glory of the ascending up of Christ the Lord that is crucified. When they heard all these words of the robber, all the holy patriarchs and prophets said with one voice: Blessed be the Lord Almighty, the Father of eternal good things, the Father of mercies, thou that hast given such grace unto thy sinners and hast brought them again into the beauty of paradise and into thy good pastures: for this is the most holy life of the spirit. Amen, Amen.

XI (XXVII)

These are the divine and holy mysteries which we saw and heard, even I, Karinus, and Leucius: but we were not suffered to relate further the rest of the mysteries of God, according as Michael the archangel strictly charged us, saying: Ye shall go with your brethren unto Jerusalem and remain in prayer, crying out and glorifying the resurrection of the Lord Jesus Christ, who hath raised you from the dead together with him: and ye shall not be speaking with any man, but sit as dumb men, until the hour come when the Lord himself suffereth you to declare the mysteries of his god head. But unto us Michael the archangel gave commandment that we should go over Jordan unto a place rich and fertile, where are many which rose again together with us for a testimony of the resurrection of Christ the Lord. For three days only were allowed unto us who rose from the dead, to keep the passover of the Lord in Jerusalem with our kindred (parents) that are living for a testimony of the resurrection of Christ the Lord: and we were baptized in the holy river of Jordan and received white robes, every one of us. And after the three days, when we had kept the passover of the Lord, all they were caught up in the clouds which had risen again with us, and were taken over Jordan and were no more seen of any man. But unto us it was said that we should remain in the city of Arimathaea and continue in prayer.

These be all things which the Lord bade us declare unto you: give praise and thanksgiving (confession) unto him, and repent that he may have mercy upon you. Peace be unto you from the same Lord Jesus Christ which is the Saviour of us all. Amen.

And when they had finished writing all things in the several volumes of paper they arose; and Karinus gave that which he had written into the hands of Annas and Caiaphas and Gamaliel; likewise Leucius gave that which he had written into the hands of Nicodemus and Joseph. And suddenly they were transfigured and became white exceedingly and were no more seen. But their writings were found to be the same (lit. equal), neither more nor less by one letter.

And when all the synagogue of the Jews heard all these marvelous sayings of Karinus and Leucius, they said one to another: Of a truth all these things were wrought by the Lord, and blessed be the Lord, world without end, Amen. And they went out all of them in great trouble of mind, smiting their breasts with fear and trembling, and departed every man unto his own home.

And all these things which were spoken by the Jews in their synagogue, did Joseph and Nicodemus forthwith declare unto the governor. And Pilate himself wrote all the things that were done and said concerning Jesus by the Jews, and laid up all the words in the public books of his judgement hall (praetorium).

XII (XXVIII)

This chapter is not found in the majority of copies.

After these things Pilate entered into the temple of the Jews and gathered together all the chief of the priests, and the teachers (grammaticos) and scribes and doctors of the law, and went in with them into the holy place of the temple and commanded all the doors to be shut, and said unto them: We have heard that ye have in this temple a certain great Bible; wherefore I ask you that it be presented before us. And when that great Bible adorned with gold and precious jewels was brought by four ministers, Pilate said to them all: I adjure you by the God of your fathers which commanded you to build this temple in the place of his sanctuary, that ye hide not the truth from me. Ye know all the things that are written in this Bible; but tell me now if ye have found in the scriptures that this Jesus whom ye have crucified is the Son of God which should come for the salvation of mankind, and in what year of the times he must come. Declare unto me whether ye crucified him in ignorance or knowingly.

And Annas and Caiaphas when they were thus adjured commanded all the rest that were will them to go out of the temple; and they themselves shut all the doors of the temple and of the sanctuary, and said unto Pilate: Thou hast adjured us, O excellent judge, by the building of this temple to make manifest unto thee the truth and reason (or a true account). After that we had crucified Jesus, knowing not that he was the Son of God, but supposing that by some chance he did his wondrous works, we made a great assembly (synagogue) in this temple; and as we conferred one with another concerning the signs of the mighty works which Jesus had done, we found many witnesses of our own nation who said that they had seen Jesus alive after his passion, and that he was passed into the height of the heaven. Moreover, we saw two witnesses whom Jesus raised from the dead, who declared unto us many marvelous things which Jesus did among the dead, which things we have in writing in our hands. Now our custom is that every year before our assembly we open this holy Bible and inquire the testimony of God. And we have found in the first book of the Seventy how that Michael the angel spake unto the third son of Adam the first man concerning the five thousand and five hundred years, wherein should come the most beloved Son of God, even Christ: and furthermore we have thought that peradventure this same was the God of Israel which said unto Moses:

Make thee an ark of the covenant in length two cubits and a half, and in breadth one cubit and a half, and in height one cubit and a half. For by those five cubits and a half we have understood and known the fashion of the ark of the old covenant, for that in five thousand and a half thousand years Jesus Christ should come in the ark of his body: and we have found that he is the God of Israel, even the Son of God. For after his passion, we the chief of the priests, because we marvelled at the signs which came to pass on his account did open the Bible, and searched out all the generations unto the generation of Joseph, and Mary the mother of Christ, taking her to be the seed of David: and we found that from the day when God made the heaven and the earth and the first man, from that time unto the Flood are 2,212 years: and from the Flood unto the building of the tower 531 years: and from the building of the tower unto Abraham 606 years: and from Abraham unto the coming of the children of Israel out of Egypt 470 years: and from the going of the children of Israel out of Egypt unto the building of the temple 511 years: and from the building of the temple unto the destruction of the same temple 464 years: so far found we in the Bible of Esdras: and inquiring from the burning of the temple unto the coming of Christ and his birth we found it to be 636 years, which together were five thousand and five hundred years like as we found it written in the Bible that Michael the archangel declared before unto Seth the third son of Adam, that after five thousand and a half thousand years Christ the Son of God hath (? should) come. Hitherto have we told no man, lest there should be a schism in our synagogues; and now, O excellent judge, thou hast adjured us by this holy Bible of the testimonies of God, and we do declare it unto thee: and we also have adjured thee by thy life and health that thou declare not these words unto any man in Jerusalem.

XIII (XXIX)

And Pilate, when he heard these words of Annas and Caiaphas, laid them all up amongst the acts of the Lord and Saviour in the public books of his judgement hall, and wrote a letter unto Claudius the king of the city of Rome, saying:

[The following Epistle or Report of Pilate is inserted in Greek into the late Acts of Peter and Paul (□ 40) and the Pseudo-Marcellus Passion of Peter and Paul (□ 19). We thus have it in Greek and Latin, and the Greek is used here as the basis of the version.]

Pontius Pilate unto Claudius, greeting.

There befell of late a matter which I myself brought to light (or made trial of): for the Jews through envy have punished themselves and their posterity with fearful judgements of their own fault; for whereas their fathers had promises (al. had announced unto them) that their God would send them out of heaven his holy one who should of right be called their king, and did promise that he would send him upon earth by a virgin; he, then (or this God of the Hebrews, then), came when I was governor of Judaea, and they beheld him enlightening the blind, cleansing lepers, healing the palsied, driving devils out of men, raising the dead, rebuking the winds, walking upon the waves of the sea dryshod, and doing many other wonders, and all the people of the Jews calling him the Son of God: the chief priests therefore, moved with envy against him, took him and delivered him unto me and brought against him one false accusation after another, saying that he was a sorcerer and did things contrary to their law.

But I, believing that these things were so, having scourged him, delivered him unto their will: and they crucified him, and when he was buried they set guards upon him. But while my soldiers watched him he rose again on the third day: yet so much was the malice of the Jews kindled that they gave money to the soldiers, saying: Say ye that his disciples stole away his body. But they, though they took the money, were not able to keep silence concerning that which had come to pass, for they also have testified that they saw him arisen and that they received money from the Jews. And these things have I reported for this cause, lest some other should lie unto thee (lat. lest any lie otherwise) and thou shouldest deem right to believe the false tales of the Jews.

Made in the USA
Lexington, KY
04 November 2010